LETTING GO
OF THE
DARKNESS!

writing my way to light

———————————

Poetry and Illustrations by
JUDY CENNAMI

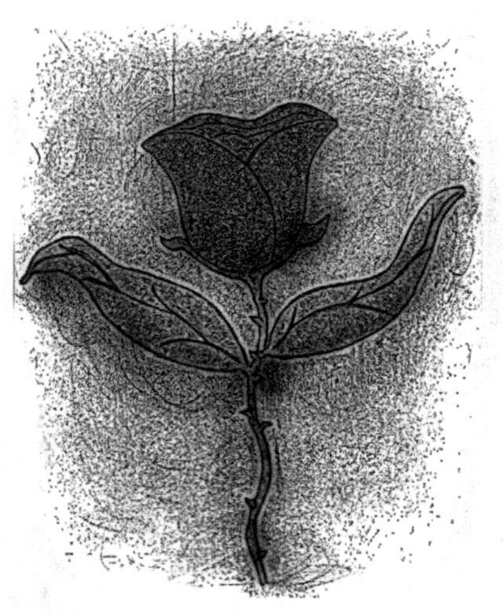

Dedication

To my sister Tabatha White,
Thank you for never giving up on me.

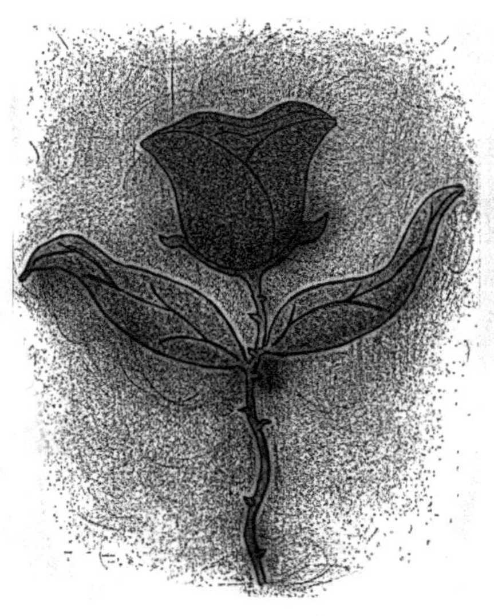

Acknowledgements

For teaching me how to change the way I think about myself and how to live a healthier lifestyle, a big THANK YOU to my sister, Tabatha White, a certified wellness coach and owner of changeyourlifestyletips.com.

To my past and present therapists and caseworkers, thank you for your support and your kindness.

And a special thank you to Ashley Black, Korie Minkus, and Lisa Vrancken. Writers of the book "BE… FROM PASSION and PURPOSE to PRODUCT and PROSPERITY". Because of you, my dreams have become my reality and for that, I thank you!

To the two wonderful individuals who were forced to read my poems and look at my drawings (you know who you are) thank you for always saying yes when I would ask: "Do you want to read my poem?" and "Do you want to see my new drawing?". You will forever have my appreciation, and my gratitude.

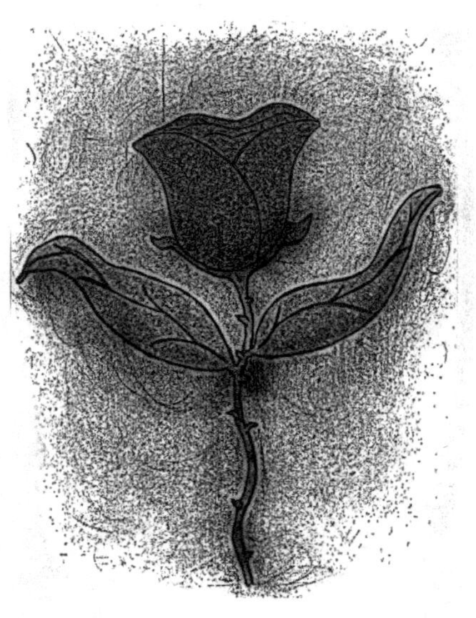

Introduction

When I was fifteen years old, I suffered from anxiety and depression. I didn't leave my house for fifteen years. I was afraid to go outside. As time passed, it only got worse. Years later, I was diagnosed with depression, anxiety, ptsd (post-traumatic stress disorder), agoraphobia and bpd (borderline personality disorder). I will not say that I "suffer" from anxiety or that I "suffer" from depression, but I will say now I am "RECOVERING" from anxiety, and now I am "RECOVERING" from depression. It has taken me years to get where I am right now. I still have a long way to go and a lot of hard work ahead of me. With the support of some great people in my life, I know I can do it.

I do not claim to be a professional poet. I do not know if you could consider what I write to be poetry. I started to write because I had a lot of thoughts running through my head, causing chaos and I needed to get them out. My poems may not make sense to everyone and that's okay. Writing these words down got the negative thoughts out of my head and it helped me get out of a lonely dark place.

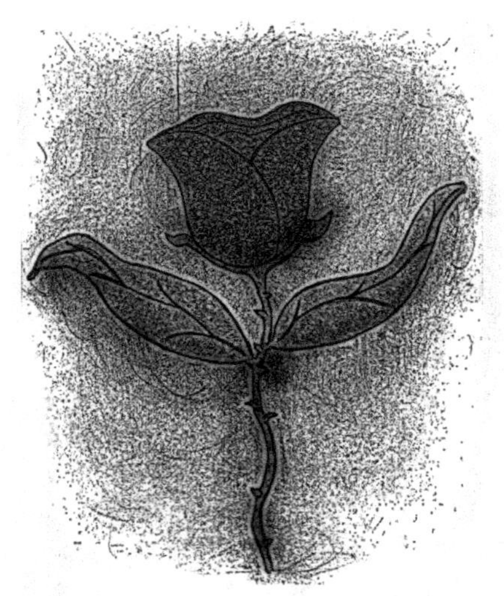

CHAPTER ONE

The Darkness

Tears of Depression

I am so tired
Tired from the unbroken torment of being me,
Being me brought forth anxiety and depression
And depression embraced the heartache of loneliness.

Loneliness has devoured my discouraged heart
My discouraged heart lost in desolation, in despair I cry,
I cry out in sorrow with silent screams
Silent screams of hidden pain.

Hidden pain trapped in mental unjust
Just fading in a whisper, yearning to die,
To die and sleep the eternal slumber
Slumber in peace, for I am so tired.

Sleepless

Blindly thrust into creation
Settled inside protective arms,
Moments later cuddled and warm
Unaware of the wickedness to come.

Not able to recognize
The beast at a glance,
He wore a cunning disguise
To conceal his existence.

Loved by many who did not notice
Feared by all with his venomous stare,
Why was I the only to see
The monster residing behind the mask.

Sleep is an illusion I must not succumb
For if my eyes fall, he will emerge.

Nightfall

Shading the light as darkness falls
Demons screeching in shadows of my mind,

A desperate need to hide to no avail
To my chagrin, I have failed.

Captive of my imagination
Thoughts of hurtful words,

Inside I feel superfluous and small
Like a scared little girl who could not shout.

Trapped

Seasons pass following your death
Yet here you are,
A figment of my imagination
Hallucination, or phantom.

Did you indeed perish
Or just desirous thinking,
Has my mind led me
To believe it true.

Awakened by the sound of a terrified scream
As my nightmares echo through the night,
Frozen by fear of a powerful presence
Am I awake, or am I dreaming?

The panic suffocates my ability to react
My impulse eager to vanish from sight,
Trapped in my nightmare without escape
I melt into the shadows of forgotten moments.

Why do you haunt me, what is it you want
You nearly destroyed me once,
But I only grew stronger
Go back to the past where you belong.

Judy Cennamo

Bottle of Emotions

Difficult to express emotion
To society I appear standoffish,
Secure I contain my feelings
They are safer in a bottle.

Set free my love repaid with hurt
Weak and bruised with invisible scars,
Strangled by worry I continue to protect
Beat up, my emotions are tender.

A crack of a smile the lid is ajar
An emotion slips out unnoticed,
Others push to the surface, I take hold
I tighten the cover once more.

The Power of Thoughts

Shadows of doubt hiding in the light
Anxiously waiting for the hours of darkness,
Ready to delve into the depths of my mind
To spread words of despair, it will loudly shout.

My screams are silent as I fight the battle
Of a war that is raging inside my head,
There is no escape
The grip is tight.

As daylight approaches, my mind in a whirl
Frantically I try to break loose
Massive in size, it separates me from the world
A wall too high, impossible to climb.

I cannot get out, and you cannot get in
I am a prisoner of my thoughts,
They hold me back
And will not let go.

I surrender to my inner turmoil
Now only emptiness, the hope is gone.

With no hesitation you approach
And with perseverance you pull me from darkness,
In your hand I see a glimmer
The key to hope, the key to my future.

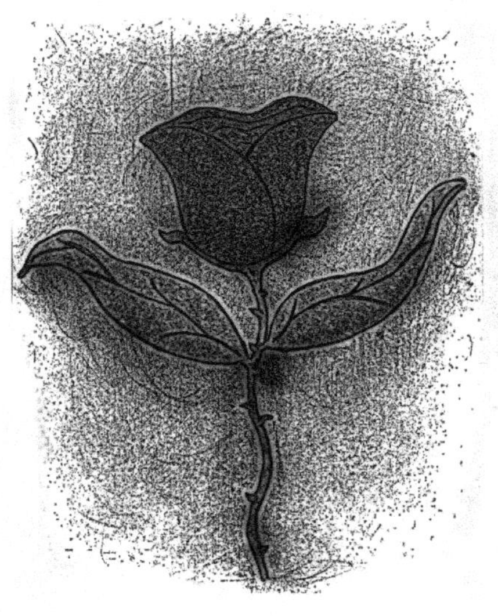

CHAPTER TWO

From The Shadows of My Mind

Forever

———

So much to say I lose my words
I wish to share what's in my heart,
We need to stop
At times we tend to drift apart.

We had our share of rough times
But together we always push through,
Because there is no better team
Than me and you.

All the good times we had together
All the memories we have made,
Just like my love for you
They will never fade.

For You

———

All alone trapped with my thoughts
Lightening fast they would swirl in my head,
An abundance of words too many to evade
My negative voice is hard to ignore.

Afraid to move forward, fear of the unknown
I slowly approach but stay at a distance,
You welcome me with your words of wisdom
And your words of support.

You've helped me more than I thought possible
No hidden assumptions, there were no judgements,
Because of that I continue to grow
For you that is why I write this poem.

Thank You

Our first meeting there was hesitation
Not knowing what to expect, my anxiety soared
Seated opposite you at the picnic table
My thoughts quieted for your friendly demeanor.

You were there for me whenever I needed
No word could describe how thankful I am,
I would not be here if not for your kindness
As well as understanding.

You helped me survive
As you helped others no doubt,
To achieve my goals I will never quit
Because of you I will continue.

Forgotten Love

It had to be fate the moment we met
There was a connection we could not deny,
You held my hand as I followed beside you
On a path unfamiliar I walk the unknown.

Spending our days discovering the world anew
Ending the night in a cozy embrace,
Feeling safe in your arms you hold me tight
Nowhere else I would rather be.

Many years have passed and look at us now
Invaded by silence our words are forced,
Now what you speak is hurtful
That echoes through my mind.

I miss the laughter where has it gone
I wish it could be the love we had,
From you three words are all I need
For me to keep fighting for a love once shared.

If Only

I yearn for the joys in life I have missed
Secluded by depression and anxiety,
Boundless pleasures slip away
For fear of being ridiculed.

Singing out loud to my favorite song
As my voice echoes within these walls,
To dance amongst the pounding words
As the melody vibrates my core of emotion.

The wind flutters around me with butterfly kisses
The sun caresses my cheek,
To walk with my dog is most enjoyable
As he sniffs every blade of grass.

Discreet glances shot my way
Pierce my inner thoughts,
As you stare you will see
The heartache and the rage.

Shame that burns around me,
A glow that is hard to miss.

Silent words are spoken
Through the eyes desolation shouts,
Sadness seeps from tired eyes
Each morn that I awaken.

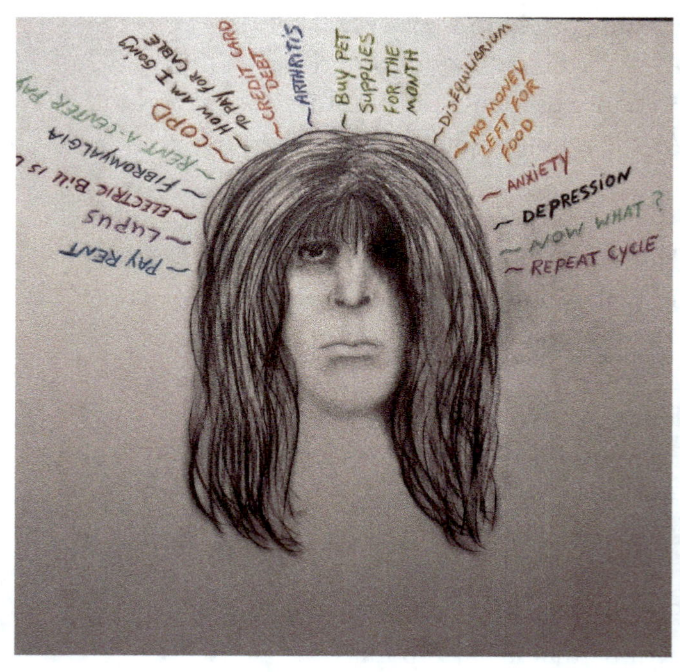
PAY RENT
LUPUS
ELECTRIC Bill is due
FIBROMYALGIA
RENT-A-CENTER PAY
COPD
HOW AM I going
to pay for CABLE
CREDIT CARD DEBT
ARTHRITIS
BUY PET SUPPLIES FOR THE MONTH
DISEQUILIBRIUM
NO MONEY LEFT FOR FOOD
ANXIETY
DEPRESSION
NOW WHAT?
REPEAT CYCLE

Why

———

Climbing out of bed is a torturous task
Why must I have this constant pain,
Why can't my body be silent and relaxed
I feel the screaming from every nerve.

Each chore gets done with agonizing steps
Why me, never have I asked before now,
Why not ask if I need a little help
Pity and sympathy I do not expect.

Why do you have to taunt me so
Bitterness is now my only friend,
Why do I let you berate me
Maybe I deserve no better.

Why do you cut me with your words
Sharp as a whip the scar is deep,
Why can't I accept a kind word for me
Not the feeling of insecurity.

As I sit here with unshed tears,
These are the thoughts that run through my head.

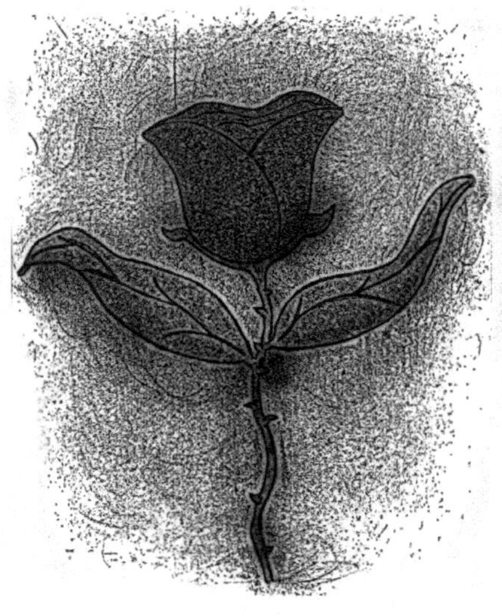

CHAPTER THREE

R. I. P.

Here with You

———————

Although unexpected
It was my time
I found peace, eternal love
In God's warm embrace, oh how he loves me so.

Wipe away those tears for me
I am standing beside you,
Whispering in your ear with love
Of memories past to calm you.

Moments you notice yourself lost
Take a minute to stop,
Close your eyes, there I'll be
To hold your hand in mine.

When you think of me, my dear
Please do not cry
My eyes will be upon you
From the heavens in the sky.

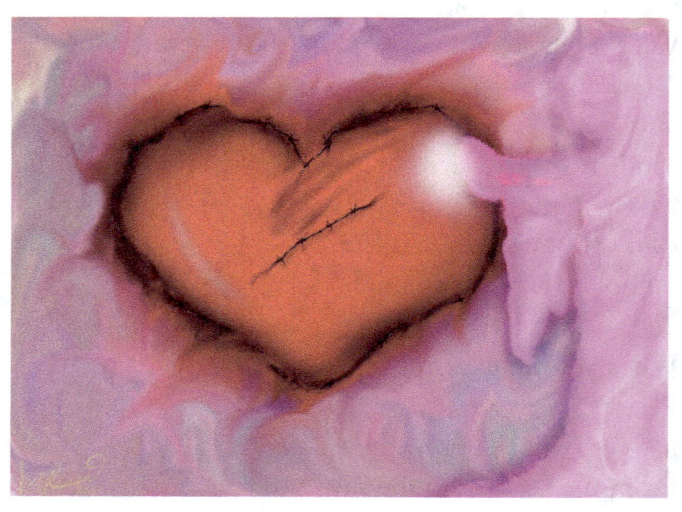

Thinking of You

Separated from this earth
You left a void that will never be filled,
At no time ignored
Forever in my heart you will stay.

Time quickly passes yet it stood still
The need to heal, the hurt is deep,
Thinking of you throughout the day
Will never forget your lovely soul.

A quiet voice I hear you speak
A message to whomever will listen,
Do not grieve for I am home
Pure love surrounds me.

Just whisper my name I'll be there
With memories to make you smile.

In your dreams I will visit
To share my love and deliver you peace,
I shall give you strength when weak
I will ease the pain of your broken heart.

Dancing with the Angels

As I look around
With hopeful eyes,
Hard not to notice
The empty feel of loss.

I try not to weep
But still they fall,
Will wipe away
These tears of mine.

Will think of you
When the sky is bright,
With an orange glow
From your shining light.

There is a heaven
For this I know,
Because there you are
Dancing with the angels.

Saying Goodbye

Wish I could see you one more time
To give you a hug and say goodbye,
I am having a hard time believing you are gone
How do I accept the loss of my friend?

I will miss the loud knock upon my front door
When you would stop by on a whim,
You whirled me away like a hurricane
With a moment's notice our wandering began.

Whether we jumped into your car to do some shopping
Or spend the day with some of your friends,
A day with you was quite the adventure
Even while sitting talking about nothing.

I can still remember the first time we met
Two hours after midnight I was sitting on my porch,
You were throwing rocks at a skunk, trying to scare him away
I told you to stop, he was doing you no harm.

As I saw you walk towards me I felt intimidated
I thought: oh my God, what did I do?
But the concern I felt was for nothing
For you had a pleasant attitude.

Admitting to me that it was wrong
You apologized and promised to never do it again,
Not for a moment did I think we would become friends
Unaware that a friendship was already forming.

Max

My heart followed behind you
Every step of your passing,
My heart will forever remain
By your side where it belongs.

The echo of your presence
Resonates within my mind,
The emptiness around me
Filled heavy with sadness.

What should I do now
For my life was yours,
Now I am lost
In this endless grief.

I miss hearing your doggie steps
As you were my house shadow,
And seeing the tilt of your head
When asked to go out.

I miss the cuddles
That you knew I needed,
Even your loud barking
I now wish to hear.

Thank you for always protecting mama
You are a good boy,
Now go run free until again we meet
And together we will be for all eternity.

It's okay, you can go, it's okay
Mama will be okay, mama will be okay.

Max and the Treat Lady

I shall cherish my friend through eternity
For whom I give title "the treat lady"

Shooting hopeful glances from across the street
As I eagerly wait for your door to open,

My tail wagging with these words from you
"Hello there, are you a good boy?"

With treats in your hand and a smile on your face
A daily routine I thoroughly enjoy.

Those peanut butter cookies were quite tasty
And on a hot day, the ice cream was splendid,

But the best treat I have received from you
Was the love you have always showered upon me.

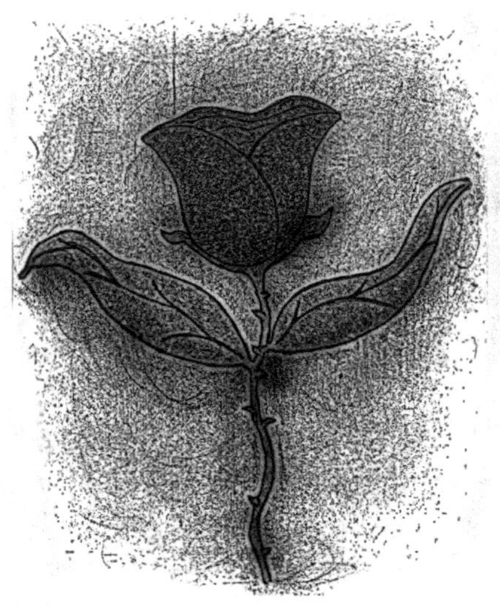

CHAPTER FOUR

FALLING INTO DARKNESS

Choices

You are the first to be seen
After he walks through the door,
From that second on
I exist no more.

He made the choice long ago
My tolerance painfully thin,
I cannot compete with you
For you will always win.

Suggestions are made for a day of fun
But then you come forth with your hissing sound,
Cracked open once again, your seal is broken
As the promises when you are around.

You alter his nature
Until he is difficult to take,
He is blind to the scheming
Of how you provoke heartache.

An ultimatum
The only thing I can do,
The hardest part to understand
Is that every occasion he chooses you.

Cursed

Numbing the ache that is possessing your core
Finding false comfort in a liquid abyss,
Desperately trying to hold onto stability
As each puncture draws you closer to death.

Spiraling uncontrollably into a private realm
Crumbling the walls of your existence,
With determination you gather the rubble
And try to build a new structure.

Your demons tucked away just below the surface
Looking for the next opportunity to come forth,
One wrong decision could reverse the course
And all your struggles would be for naught.

You are on a roller coaster heading uphill
Suddenly the track plummets and all is lost,
Restore the track in a new direction
And leave behind the toxic passenger.

Search deep for the cause of your distress
To calm the monster within,
Be proud of today and all you have accomplished
Do not dwell on what is past.

The Frumpy Slipper

A fool I have become to others
They see how swiftly I am being replaced,
Your denial is constant
You believe it truth.

An old tattered slipper you tossed me aside
With no concern of the hurt inflicted
Forgotten, rejected, collecting dust,
You gained a new favorite with cushion aplenty.

Quiet footsteps getting louder
He is coming! He did not forget!
The blow of disappointment hits me hard
From the breeze of his passing hand.

Years of adjustment for the perfect fit
Does he not know how we formed together,
Every bump and curve
Softened his walk.

Unwanted and worthless I have become to you
With no hesitation you threw me away,
Buried deep the heaviness grows
Until I receive a tug that pulls me from cluster.

Appearing ragged upon the surface
But underneath has value,
Someone else will choose what you discarded
The warmth on a frosty night.

Lost

———

Peering through eyes
That once sparkled,
Now weeping with sorrow
Turning to ice.

With each teardrop
Flowing within,
Emotions becoming numb
I slowly die.

Emotions drained
Forever lost,
I exist no more
Inside I am dead.

I glance at you
Through new eyes,
And see the truth
That cannot be denied.

Lost Hope

I drown in sorrow
Held tight with despair,
Eager for happiness
Never found.

Hands of kindness reached out to me
My spirit awakens from a timeless slumber,
A friendship emerges, we acknowledge love
Forever companions or so I thought.

Growing old together is my illusion
You rumpled my heart and tossed into desolation,
Again aloneness has fallen upon me
Heartache has become my only friend.

To allow the hope to infiltrate
Will bring forth immense disaster,
Must strengthen the wall before it rubbles
Shield from emotional unrest.

Changes

Separate roads following nineteen years
Into the unknown I must walk alone,
Reservations stemming from my fears
I must find the courage to gather my own.

Never faltering was my loyalty to you,
Whilst your loyalties now belong to another,
You can deny and say it's not true
As you are with some other.

Slowly dying inside as each day passes
The ache dwells on a permanent scar,
The tears easily flowing
Wondering how things ever got this far.

You made your choice
Now I have to decide mine,
I will not raise my voice
Nor will I pretend it to be fine.

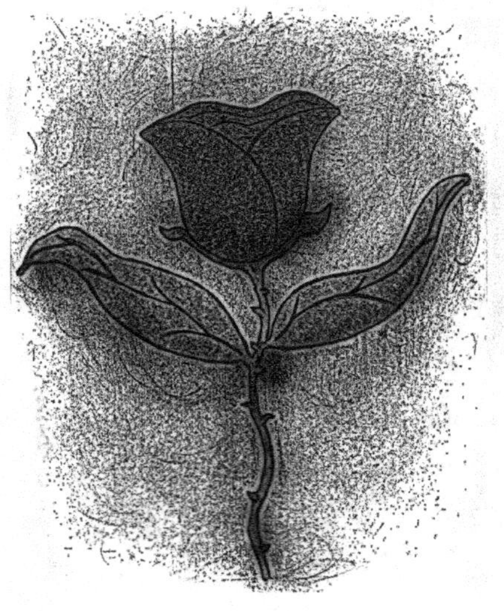

CHAPTER FIVE

A Shimmer of Light

Finding My Way

I cannot envision
My future path,
For the road is hidden
Behind the fog.

My mind will not venture
To what could be,
Or what I can achieve
For I do not know.

My spirit lost
Amongst my thoughts,
I search for myself
Within that chaos.

To set future goals
I find impossible,
For each day that I get through
Is a goal accomplished.

BOOK of my POEMS
THE POSSIBILITIES ARE ENDLESS!
?

Goals

———

For each small goal
There is a reward,
The satisfaction
Of one achieved.

For each achievement
That is accomplished,
One step closer
A step further away.

For each step taken
One is left behind,
No turning back
On a forward motion.

For the forward motion
Down the road,
A reward awaits
From each small goal.

Recovery

The eye of madness blinded by confidence
No words of mock to hold me captive,
As I cross the threshold into recovery
The artistry of nature prepares to bloom.

Flames of the sun throws gentle caresses
Embraced by the warmth of a dancing breeze.

The majestic tree stands tall to protect
Nourishes the wild and shelters the lost
Birds, squirrels, and tiny insects,
Provider of creatures big and small.

My awareness consumes
Wonderment far and wide,
Without fear of ridicule
Deceiving my mind.

Judy Cennamo
1-10-2018

Self-Portrait

A poem regarding my good qualities
Will be quite the challenge,
What makes me happy, what are my passions?

A listening ear that understands
I will give advice when I can,
A comforting shoulder to catch the tears
To absorb the trickle of sadness.

I can make you smile
That sends a chuckle within,
Producing a tickle in the chest
Causing laughter to explode.

I see the good qualities in everyone I meet
Never ignore what I see beneath,
I do not judge on one's appearance
For each imperfection has a story.

I am a tough cookie so I have been told
Fighting my battles I remain strong,
Win or lose I will never give up
The fighter in me emerges.

I admit that I am a perfectionist
Rewarding at times but also frustrating,
My passions are to draw and write these poems
To get lost in creative stimulation.

Here you go my poem is done
I hope you enjoyed the read,
As much as I enjoyed the write.

Fighting Myself

I see you have returned
When the desire to die,
Is stronger than
The will to live.

I could choose a remedy
But my happiness would be fake,
And to tell myself that I will thrive
But deep down know it is a lie.

I could pretend to be
Someone with life,
But eventually the real me
Always claims her spot.

But maybe the real me
Is the one with life,
Buried long ago
Now fighting her way out.

Shovel in hand
I remove the dirt,
Reaching in I grab her tightly
I will help her to emerge.

Home

Too intense my emotions
For this unkind world,
Of this earth
I did not belong.

The search for happiness
Never grasped,
The need to feel loved
Never felt.

The broken pieces
That never quite fit,
For of this earth
I did not belong.

Love for my family
I have never shown,
Unbeknownst to them
They reside in my heart.

For each achievement
Accomplished by you,
That moment is captured
On canvas by me.

My soul is shining
I am finally home,
Because this earth
I did not belong.

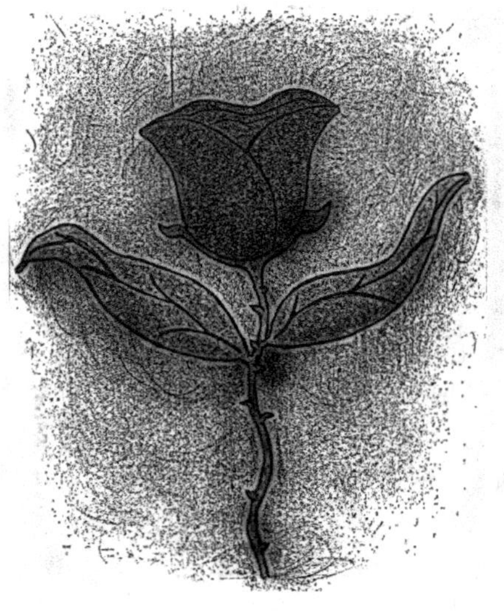

2021: MY LIFE BEGINS!

I know my last poem did not end on a good note. That is because I still struggle with these thoughts. I am not going to lie, every day is still a battle for me. I have always felt that I did not deserve to be happy. I have always felt that I did not deserve to be loved. There are days that I still feel that way, but I am working on it. I will keep fighting for myself and fight for that life I deserve, a life that I was meant to have. This is one battle that I am determined to win! Enough of the bad, let's get into the good.

Things are going pretty good right now, I am starting to feel good about myself. I smoked for 40 years and decided I wanted to stop. It wasn't easy but after many attempts I was finally able to quit. Now I am free! I say I am free because I was a prisoner of those cigarettes. I am eating healthier, even just eating for that matter (I have a bad habit of punishing myself by not eating). Okay I got off track. My mind does that sometimes, keeps going to the bad. I'm working on that too.

Back to the good. In January 2021, I made a vision board and I had three goals on it. My first goal was to have an online store. I built and created my own website where I sell my artwork on various products.

First goal accomplished! My second goal was to have my poetry published. I did not have the money for a publisher, so I decided to create an illustrated poetry book and publish it myself. As you can see by reading this book my Second goal has been accomplished! My third goal is to have my own house. This one has not been accomplished yet, but I am hoping that it will be some day. It still amazes me how when you put your mind to something, you can accomplish anything. And one day I will get my house. I have no doubt about that.

Drawing is my passion and for years I gave it up for depression and anxiety, but never again will depression and anxiety take away what I love. For all of those lost years I have given them power, well I am taking back that power. I am in control now, not them.

Thank you for taking the time to read this book and sharing this journey with me. I hope that you enjoyed it as much as I enjoyed creating it for you. I also hope that it touches some of you in a way that makes you realize that you too can come out of the darkness and into the light and find the joy in life as I did.

THE FOLLOWING PAGES CONTAIN

ADDITIONAL ARTWORK

By

JUDY CENNAMI

And can be found at

JudyblueArt.com

And also on instagram

@judyblueart

Judy Clare - Art

Judy Glue · Art

Judy Glue . Art

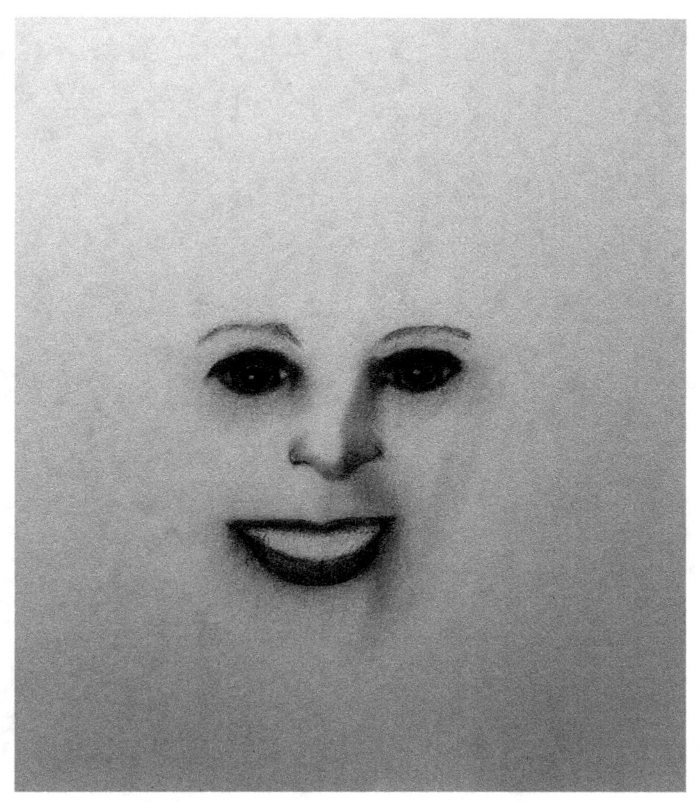

Judy Glue Art

Judy Glue · Art

Index of Poems